MEGA BOOKS

# TRUCKS

DEBORAH MURRELL
AND CHRISTIANE GUNZI

Gareth Stevens
PUBLISHING

# BE A SUPER SPOTTER

Study these pictures and look out for them as you read this book. Can you answer the super spotter questions?

**Which truck has these flames?**

**Which truck moves on these tracks?**

**Which truck has these stars?**

**Which truck is lifting these logs?**

**Please visit our website, www.garethstevens.com. For a free color catalog of all our high-quality books, call toll free 1-800-542-2595 or fax 1-877-542-2596.**

Published in 2025 by
**Gareth Stevens Publishing**
2544 Clinton St.
Buffalo, NY 14224



Written and edited by: Deborah Murrell and Christiane Gunzi
Designer: Paul Calver
Design assistance: Ray Bryant & Gill Shaw
Commercial vehicle consultant: Peter J. Davies
Education consultants: Diana Bentley, MA Advanced Diploma in Children's Literature;
Jane Whitwell, Diploma in Special Educational Needs

Caterpillar; Daimler Chrysler Ltd; Ford Motor Company; Freightliner Group; Leibherr (manufacturer of the world's largest range of mobile cranes); McNeilus; Oshkosh Truck Corporation, Oshkosh, Wisconsin USA; Scania Image Desk



**Cataloging-in-Publication Data**

Names: Murrell, Deborah. | Gunzi, Christiane.
Title: Trucks / by Deborah Murrell and Christiane Gunzi.
Description: Buffalo, NY : Gareth Stevens Publishing, 2025. | Series: Mega books
Identifiers: ISBN 9781482468144 (pbk.) | ISBN 9781482468151 (library bound) | ISBN 9781482468168 (ebook)
Subjects: LCSH: Trucks--Juvenile literature.
Classification: LCC TL230.15 M87 2025 | DDC 629.224--dc23



Printed in the United States of America

CPSIA compliance information: Batch #CSGS25: For further information contact Gareth Stevens at 1-800-542-2595.

Find us on

# CONTENTS

# TRANSPORTERS

There is a different sort of truck for every job. Some big trucks are used for carrying cars, food, or animals from one place to another. These kinds of trucks are called transporters.

A long-distance articulated truck

## Rigid trucks

This red truck is called a rigid truck because it cannot bend. Its driver has to be very good at driving around corners.

### Can you point to?

a wheel

a mirror

some lights

a grille

# Bendy trucks

Trucks that can bend are called articulated trucks. A bendy truck is quite easy to drive around corners. This articulated transporter is carrying some cars and pickup trucks.

A car transporter

## What colors are these transporters?

# LOGGERS

Trucks that carry logs are called loggers. A logger is big, tough, and powerful. It has to pull hundreds of logs in its trailer over rough, muddy tracks.

## Hold tight

There are strong posts along each side of the trailer to keep all of the logs in place.

# Why is this logger so big?

## Harvester

This truck's long arm has a tool on the end called a harvester. It holds the tree while a sharp saw cuts through the wood.

## Loader

This little loader picks up the logs and lifts them onto the trailer.

# MIGHTY TRUCKS

In some countries, there are massive trucks that can pull two, three, or even four trailers. These mighty trucks are called road trains. Road trains often carry their loads for thousands of miles!

## Can you point to?

a circle

a diamond

a rectangle

some triangles

## Twin trailers

This mega truck has two trailers joined together. It is called a B-double outfit.

**Can you count the wheels on the road train?**

## Carrying fuel

This long road train is transporting huge fuel tanks on three trailers.

# DIGGERS

Trucks called diggers are specially made for digging. They have different kinds of buckets for digging up different things. Some buckets are strong enough to cut through hard rock!

## Up and over

This digger has a loader arm that reaches over the top of the cab. A wire cage protects the driver as the digger tips its load out of the bucket.

## Tracks

This digger has tracks instead of wheels. The tracks help the digger to move safely over slippery surfaces.

## Why are the tracks useful?

## A strong arm

The driver controls the digger's arm from inside the cab. The arm picks up its load in the bucket and drops it in the right place.

# BIG BULLDOZER

Bulldozers are used for clearing the ground to get it ready for building. This enormous bulldozer can cut through almost anything. It pushes everything out of the way as it rumbles along.

## Big bucket

This huge bucket has a sharp metal blade which can even cut through tree trunks.

## Can you point to?

a grille

a sprocket

a number

# What is this bulldozer used for?

## A good grip

The tracks on the bulldozer help it to grip, so it can climb up steep slopes too.

# LOADERS

Trucks that load things into other trucks are called loaders. They have a short, strong arm for lifting. A loader can carry heavy rubble in its bucket.

## Filling the tipper

The loader is emptying its big bucket of soil into the back of a red tipper truck. The loader can fill up the truck very quickly.

## A huge load

This loader has forks instead of a bucket. It is carrying a heavy chunk of chalk. Diggers dig the chalk out of the ground.

## Why does a loader have big tires?

### Chunky tires

Loaders often have wide tires. Big tires help to stop the loader from falling over.

# GIANT DUMPER

Enormous dumpers are used in quarries. They carry huge loads of rock from where they are dug out of the ground. This mega dump truck is as big as a house!

## Wow!

These children are three years old. See how tiny they are next to this mega truck!

# What does a dumper do?

## Can you point to?

a sign

air filters

a ladder

## Super size

The cab is so high off the ground that the driver has to climb up a ladder to get inside.

## Bit by bit

This dumper is so gigantic that it cannot drive along ordinary roads. Other trucks have to take it to the site one piece at a time.

# CONCRETE MIXERS

Trucks called concrete mixers collect concrete in their drum and carry it to building sites. The big drum goes around and around all the time to mix the concrete and keep it liquid!

A small white concrete mixer

What pattern is on the big drum?

## Extra wheels

This mixer has extra wheels on the back. The driver lowers these wheels when the mixer is traveling on public roads to the building site.

# At the site

When a mixer arrives at the building site, the concrete is poured out of the back of the drum. It slides down a long chute, ready to use for building.

# TIPPERS

These trucks are called tippers. They are used for delivering sand, gravel, and other building materials to building sites. When tippers empty their loads, they tip up sideways or backward.

**An end tipper**

## Side tipper

This white tipper has a body that can tip up sideways to deliver its load of wood chips.

**What does a tipper do?**

## Which of these trucks is a side tipper?

### Can you point to?

a mud flap

a ram

a mirror

some lights

## Tipping up

The front of this yellow end tipper lifts up so that its load of earth can slide off the back.

# ROAD BUILDERS

Building a new road takes a long time. There are lots of things to do before the asphalt goes on top. All of these machines have their own special jobs.

## Roller

This big roller is very heavy. It rolls along the road to make it flat.

## Scraper

This truck is a scraper. It scrapes the top layer of soil off the ground so that the road can be put on top.

# What job does a grader do?

## Grader

This machine is called a grader. It helps to make the ground all smooth before the road is built.

# Which machine makes the road flat?

# GARBAGE TRUCKS

Garbage trucks help to keep all the streets clean and tidy. They collect everyone's garbage and take it away.

**A back loader**

## Can you see a garbage tote?

## Front loader

This yellow garbage truck has two arms on the front that can lift up heavy dumpsters full of garbage.

A blue side-loading garbage truck

## Side loader

This blue garbage truck has an arm on the side for picking up big garbage totes. The arm grabs the tote, lifts it up, and empties the garbage into the truck.

# MEGA CRANES

Powerful cranes like this one are called mobile cranes. They have special steering and can travel on roads and over rough ground. Mobile cranes are used on all kinds of building sites.

## Superstrong

This giant crane can lift heavy loads high off the ground and move them safely to another place.

# What are cranes used for?

## On the move

The jib of this mobile crane folds down and lies on top of the cab when the crane is traveling along the road.

## Can you point to?

an exhaust

a light

some chevrons

a pulley

# TOUGH TRUCKS

Army trucks are strong and powerful. They have to be able to drive over rocks, mud, and sand, as well as on ordinary roads. Some army trucks can also drive through deep water!

**An army truck traveling across a river**

**Can you see a clean spare tire?**

## Carrying a container

This truck is loading a big container onto its back. The driver can control the lifting arm from inside the cab.

## Tough front

Army trucks are extra tough at the front. They can easily push their way through walls and fences.

# MONSTER TRUCKS

These huge pickup trucks are specially made for racing and jumping. People enjoy watching them do tricks at shows. Monster trucks are so wide that they are not allowed on ordinary roads.

A monster truck called Blue Thunder

A Bigfoot truck

## Biggest truck

This monster truck is called Bigfoot 5. It is the tallest, widest, heaviest pickup truck in the whole world!

## Wow!

These children are three years old. See how tiny they are next to this truck!

## Jumping truck

Monster trucks are used to jump over old cars, just for fun. They are so tough that they crush the cars when they land on them.

**Why do people drive jumping trucks?**

# GLOSSARY

**Articulated** – a truck that has two or more sections that are joined together by a flexible joint.

**Building site** – a place where houses, apartments, or other structures are being built.

**Cab** – the place in a truck where the driver sits. Also called a cabin.

**Chute** – a slide or big tube that allows things, such as sand or bricks, to be moved to a lower level or to the ground.

**Concrete** – a building material made from a mixture of sand, stone or gravel, cement, and water. It can be spread or poured when wet, but once it sets it is hard and very strong.

**Container** – a large metal box that can be carried on the back of a truck or on a ship. They are used to transport things easily and safely over long distances.

**Crane** – a big, tall machine that is used to lift or move heavy or large objects.

**Jib** – the "arm" of a crane.

**Pickup truck** – a truck with a covered cab and an area at the back that has low sides. They are used for carrying loads that might not easily fit in an ordinary car or van.

**Quarry** – a place where rock, sand, slate, or other natural materials are dug out of the ground.

**Rigid** – something that is hard or fixed in place is rigid.

# INDEX